THE
WILDERNESS
EXPERIENCE

CALL OF THE RIVER

WRITINGS AND PHOTOGRAPHS

SELECTED AND EDITED BY

PAGE STEGNER

A Harvest Original
HARCOURT BRACE & COMPANY
SAN DIEGO • NEW YORK • LONDON

A TEHABI BOOK

Copyright © 1996 by Tehabi Books

Wendell Berry, excerpt "The Rise" from *Recollected Essays 1965-1980,* by Wendell Berry. Copyright © 1981 by Wendell Berry. Reprinted by permission from Farrar, Straus & Giroux.

Gretel Ehrlich, excerpt from *Islands, the Universe, Home,* by Gretel Ehrlich. Copyright © 1991 by Gretel Ehrlich. Used by permission of Viking Penguin, a division of Penguin Books USA Inc.

Barry Lopez, excerpt "The Shallows" from *River Notes* by Barry Holstun Lopez. Copyright © 1979 by Barry Holstun Lopez. Reprinted with permission by Sterling Lord Literistic, Inc.

Patrick F. McManus, from *The Grasshopper Trap* by Patrick F. McManus. Copyright © 1985 by Patrick F. McManus. Reprinted by permission of Henry Holt and Co., Inc.

Harry Middleton, "Midnight's Rivers," excerpted from *Rivers of Memory,* by Harry Middleton. Copyright © 1993 by Harry Middleton. Reprinted with permission in its abridged form by Pruett Publishing Company, Boulder, Colorado.

Wallace Stegner, from *The Sound of Mountain Water,* by Wallace Stegner. Copyright © 1969 by Wallace Stegner. Used by permission of Doubleday, a division of Bantam Doubleday Dell Publishing Group, Inc.

Ann Zwinger, excerpt "Lower Green River Lake to Kendall Warm Springs" from *Run, River, Run* by Ann Zwinger. Copyright © 1975 by Ann Zwinger. Published 1975 by Harper & Row and University of Arizona Press. Reprinted with permission in its abridged form by Frances Collin, Literary Agent.

Library of Congress Cataloging-in-Publication Data

Call of the river: writings and photographs / selected and edited by Page Stegner. — 1st ed.

    p. cm.— (The wilderness experience)

"A Harvest original."

"A Tehabi book."

ISBN 0-15-600227-2 (pbk.)

1. Natural history—United States.   2. Rivers—United States.   3. United States—Discription and travel.
4. Natural history—United States—Pictorial works.   5. Rivers—United States—Pictorial works.   6. United States—Pictorial works.
I. Stegner, Page.   II. Series.

QH104.C3 1996

508.73—dc20

96-13561
CIP

Call of the River was conceived and produced by Tehabi Books. Nancy Cash–*Series Editor and Developmental Editor;* Laura Georgakakos–*Manuscript Editor;* Kathi George-*Copy Proofer;* Andy Lewis–*Art Director;* Sam Lewis–*Art Director;* Tom Lewis–*Editorial and Design Director;* Sharon Lewis–*Controller;* Chris Capen–*President.*

Illustrations by Thomas G. Lewis

Harcourt Brace & Company and Tehabi Books, in association with The Basic Foundation, a not-for-profit organization whose primary mission is reforestation, will facilitate the planting of two trees for every one tree used in the manufacture of this book. This edition is printed on acid-free paper that meets the American National Standards Institute Z39.48 Standard.

Printed in Hong Kong through Mandarin Offset.
First edition 1996
A B C D E

CONTENTS

Call of the River
Introduction
by Page Stegner
1

Symphony of the Stream
From *The Sound of Mountain Water*
by Wallace Stegner
9

River Rising
Excerpts from *Recollected Essays 1965–1980*
by Wendell Berry
17

Water in Wildness
Excerpts from *Islands, the Universe, Home*
by Gretel Ehrlich
27

White-water Warrior
Snaggletooth
by Page Stegner
37

River Stones
Excerpts from *River Notes*
by Barry Lopez
49

Shadows and Silence
The Night River
by Kathleen Dean Moore
59

Sidestepping Downstream
Excerpts from *Run, River, Run*
by Ann Zwinger
69

The Old Fishin' Hole
From *The Grasshopper Trap*
by Patrick F. McManus
79

Of Dreams and Rivers
Excerpts from *Rivers of Memory*
by Harry Middleton
91

About the Photographers and the Photographs
100

CALL OF THE RIVER

The call of the river is a complexity of motion and sound which extracts from mere mortals the wildest diversity of emotional response. Awe, dread, tranquility, devotion, ecstasy. The river is an abstraction of universal force. It moves mountains, levels plains, cuts mile-deep canyons down through the history of geological time. It is all power and mystery. In the murmur and burble of its flow it comforts the most unquiet soul; in the thunder of its cataracts it can put the fear of God in the most courageous spirit. The river is all harmony and chaos, and it is just as impassive and deadly as it is voluble and bright. No wonder it inspires reflection.

If the essays in this book have anything in common it is the celebration of what one might call the "life" of a river. I do not mean organic life, I mean something metaphysical and abstract, a ubiquitous force detectable in the intricate choreography and musicology of flowing water, in its song and dance if you will. Every river performs a unique and distinct ballet, but the sum and substance of every one is always the same—a divine expression of uncompromising energy.

Of course, a symbiosis is required. In order to hear the poetry one must have a poetic ear, to really see the dance one must take off the dark glasses. As this century rushes toward conclusion there seem fewer and fewer (at least in relative terms) who will take the time to watch and listen. As Aldo Leopold once said, "One of the facts hewn to by science [by which he meant industry, progress, materialism] is that every river needs more people, and all people need more inventions, and hence more science; the good life depends on the indefinite extension of this chain of logic. That the good life on any river may likewise depend on the perception of its music, and the preservation of some music to perceive, is a form of doubt not yet entertained by science."

The authors in this collection are among the very best of the many contemporary American writers who have devoted a significant part of their literary careers to perceiving the music of the natural environment and to transcribing it for the rest of us. They are some of my favorites, though given space enough and time I could have included many others of whom I am equally

1

fond—Ted Hoagland, Ed Abbey, John Daniel, John McPhee, Tom Watkins, Bill McKibben, Diane Ackerman, to name only a few.

When I say these writers have devoted a significant part of their careers to the contemplation of man's relationship with his surroundings, I do not mean to suggest that the preponderance of their work is "nature writing" or that their performance in that particular arena represents their major contribution to literature in general. The power and eloquence of a Wendell Berry, Wallace Stegner, Barry Lopez, Gretel Ehrlich is at least in part a consequence of skills each has developed over the years as a novelist, short story writer, and/or poet. But whatever the genre, and whatever formal training in the natural sciences they may have had, the unifying factor—one shared by all the writers represented here—is a superb eye for detail, a keen ear for language, and a fertile imagination.

Given the current enthusiasm among many members of the 104th Congress to further silence the "music of rivers," to turn our public wildlands into oil fields, strip mines, clear-cuts, and housing developments, I am tempted, in sour moments, to feel that this book may be a kind of eulogy. A remembrance of things past. "The life of every river sings its own song," says Leopold, "but in most the song is long since marred by the discords of misuse."

Already every major river in this country has been dammed, diverted, apportioned, and harnessed to power generation. Take the mighty Missouri. Only for a stretch of 208 miles in Montana does that 2,700-mile water course resemble its once majestic, free-flowing past. Take the Colorado. The "river no more," to borrow Philip Fradkin's phrase, is so massively controlled by dams and so totally apportioned to the seven upper and lower basin states (plus a teacup to Mexico) that nothing has flowed out of its mouth into the Gulf of California for twenty-five years.

The same story of conquest is repeated for the Delaware River, the Connecticut, the Tennessee, the Arkansas, the Columbia, the Snake, the Rio Grande, the Sacramento, and so on and so on and so on. The once great web of free-flowing rivers across our continent is *absolutely* a remembrance of things past, though we have preserved in the Wild and Scenic Rivers System short portions of something over sixty—twenty-six of which are in Alaska. That's not much pristine riparian corridor for 250 million people to escape to for the kind of rejuvenation described in the pages of this book. And you can be sure every freshet, spring, seep, trickle, rivulet, runnel, and rill that hasn't yet been exploited is under scrutiny by somebody who would like to.

In lighter moments, I think of this book as antidote. Even if the joy of a contemplative merging into the riverbank landscape is here vicarious, it inspires future action and response. These marvelous evocations, these private moments, perhaps best described as confrontations with a divine spirit, may help us to see for ourselves what is in the wave other than water, may help us to listen for, and to hear, the music. Take a Zwinger and Moore with breakfast, a Middleton after dinner, and a McManus before bed. Call me in the morning. —*Page Stegner*

SYMPHONY OF THE STREAM

In this short chapter from The Sound of Mountain Water, *a collection of essays on the changing American West, my father, Wallace Stegner, offers a glimpse into the origins of a sensibility that enabled him to become the most eloquent and widely recognized voice in this century to speak on behalf of wildness and its preservation. —P. S.*

From *The Sound of Mountain Water* by

WALLACE STEGNER

I discovered mountain rivers late, for I was a prairie child, and knew only flatland and dryland until we toured the Yellowstone country in 1920, loaded with all the camp beds, auto tents, grub-boxes, and auxiliary water and gas cans that 1920 thought necessary. Our road between Great Falls, Montana, and Salt Lake City was the rutted track that is now Highway 89. Beside a marvelous torrent, one of the first I ever saw, we camped several days. That was Henry's Fork of the Snake.

I didn't know that it rose on the west side of Targhee Pass and flowed barely a hundred miles, through two Idaho counties, before joining the Snake near Rexburg; or that in 1810 Andrew Henry built on its bank near modern St. Anthony the first American post west of the Continental Divide. The divide itself meant nothing to me. My imagination was not stretched by the wonder of the parted waters, the Yellowstone rising only a few miles eastward to flow out toward the Missouri, the Mississippi, the Gulf, while this bright pounding stream was starting through its thousand miles of canyons to the Columbia and the Pacific.

All I knew was that it was pure delight to be where the land lifted in peaks and plunged in canyons, and to sniff air thin, spray-cooled, full of pine and spruce smells, and to be so close-seeming to the improbable indigo sky. I gave my heart to the mountains the minute I stood beside this river with its spray in my face and watched it thunder into foam, smooth to green glass over

9

sunken rocks, shatter to foam again. I was fascinated by how it sped by and yet was always there; its roar shook both the earth and me.

When the sun dropped over the rim the shadows chilled sharply; evening lingered until foam on the water was ghostly and luminous in the near-dark. Alders caught in the current sawed like things alive, and the noise was louder. It was rare and comforting to waken late and hear the undiminished shouting of the water in the night. And at sunup it was still there, powerful and incessant, with the slant sun tangled in its rainbow spray, the grass blue with wetness, and the air heady as ether and scented with campfire smoke.

By such a river it is impossible to believe that one will ever be tired or old. Every sense applauds it. Taste it, feel its chill on the teeth: it is purity absolute. Water its racing current, its steady renewal of force: it is transient and eternal. And listen again to its sounds: get far enough away so that the noise of falling tons of water does not stun the ears, and hear how much is going on underneath—a whole symphony of smaller sounds, hiss and splash and gurgle, the small talk of side channels, the whisper of blown and scattered spray gathering itself and beginning to flow again, secret and irresistible, among the wet rocks. ❧

RIVER RISING

There is a majestic power in the flow of a river that transcends our capacity to conceive and remember—something, as Wendell Berry puts it, that both fascinates and horrifies. A river, like all natural forces, is not indifferent or unresponsive to humankind (words which imply intent), it is simply "not subject." This excerpt from Recollected Essays 1965–1980 *is a small example of why Edward Abbey called Berry the "best essayist now working in America." —P. S.*

Excerpts from *Recollected Essays 1965–1980* by
WENDELL BERRY

We put the canoe in about six miles up the Kentucky River from my house. There, at the mouth of Drennon Creek, is a little colony of summer camps. We knew we could get down to the water there with some ease. And it proved easier than we expected. The river was up maybe twenty feet, and we found a path slanting down the grassy slope in front of one of the cabins. It went right into the water, as perfect for launching the canoe and getting in as if it had been worn there by canoeists.

To me that is the excitement of a rise: the unexpectedness, always, of the change it makes. What was difficult becomes easy. What was easy becomes difficult. By water, what was distant becomes near. By land, what was near becomes distant. At the waterline, when a rise is on, the world is changing. There is an irresistible sense of adventure in the difference. Once the river is out of its banks, a vertical few inches of rise may widen the surface by many feet over the bottomland. A sizable lagoon will appear in the middle of a cornfield. A drain in a pasture will become a canal. Stands of beech and oak will take on the look of a cypress swamp. There is something Venetian about it. There is a strange excitement in going in a boat where one would ordinarily go on foot—or where, ordinarily, birds would be flying. And so the first excitement of our trip was that little path; where it might go in a time of low water was unimaginable. Now it went down to the river.

17

Because of the offset in the shore at the creek mouth, there was a large eddy turning in the river where we put in, and we began our drift downstream by drifting upstream. We went up inside the row of shore trees, whose tops now waved in the current, until we found an opening among the branches, and then turned out along the channel. The current took us. We were still settling ourselves as if in preparation, but our starting place was already diminishing behind us.

There is something ominously like life in that. One would always like to settle oneself, get braced, say "Now I am going to begin"—and then begin. But as the necessary quiet seems about to descend, a hand is felt at one's back, shoving. And that is the way with the river when a current is running: once the connection with the shore is broken, the journey has begun.

We were, of course, already at work with the paddles. But we were ahead of ourselves. I think that no matter how deliberately one moved from the shore into the sudden violence of a river on the rise, there would be bound to be several uneasy minutes of transition. It is another world, which means that one's senses and reflexes must begin to live another kind of life. Sounds and movements that from the standpoint of the shore might have come to seem even familiar now make a new urgent demand on the attention. There is everything to get used to, from a wholly new perspective. And from the outset one has the currents to deal with.

It is easy to think, before one has ever tried it, that nothing could be easier than to drift down the river in a canoe on a strong current. That is because when one thinks of a river one is apt to think of *one* thing—a great singular flowing that one puts one's boat into and lets go. But it is not like that at all, not after the water is up and the current swift. It is not one current, but a braiding together of several, some going at different speeds, some even in different directions. Of course, one *could* just let go, let the boat be taken into the continuous mat of drift—leaves, logs, whole trees, cornstalks, cans, bottles, and such—in the channel, and turn and twist in the eddies there. But one does not have to do that long in order to sense the helplessness of a light canoe when it is sideways to the current. It is out of control then, and endangered. Stuck in the mat of drift, it can't be maneuvered. It would turn over easily; one senses that by a sort of ache in the nerves, the way bad footing is sensed. And so we stayed busy, keeping the canoe between the line of half-submerged shore trees and the line of drift that marked the channel. We weren't trying to hurry—the currents were carrying us as fast as we wanted to go—but it took considerable labor just to keep straight. It was like riding a spirited horse not fully bridle-wise: We kept our direction *by intention*; there could be no dependence on habit or inertia; when our minds wandered the river took over and turned us according to inclinations of its own. It bore us like a consciousness, acutely wakeful, filling perfectly the lapses in our own.

But we did grow used to it, and accepted our being on it as one of the probabilities, and began to take the mechanics of it for granted. The necessary sixth sense had come to us, and we began to notice more than we had to.

There is an exhilaration in being *accustomed* to a boat on dangerous water. It is as though into one's consciousness of the dark violence of the depths at one's feet there rises the idea of the boat, the buoyancy of it. It is always with a sort of triumph that the boat is realized—that it goes *on top of the water*, between breathing and drowning. It is an ancient-feeling triumph; it must have been one of the first ecstasies. The analogy of riding a spirited horse is fairly satisfactory; it is mastery over something resistant—a buoyancy that is not natural and inert like that of a log, but desired and vital and to one's credit. Once the boat has fully entered the consciousness it becomes an intimate extension of the self; one feels as competently amphibious as a duck. And once we felt accustomed and secure in the boat, the day and the river began to come clear to us.

It was a gray, cold Sunday in the middle of December. In the woods on the north slopes above us we could see the black trunks and branches just faintly traced with snow, which gave them a silvery, delicate look—the look of impossibly fine handwork that nature sometimes has. And they looked cold. The wind was coming straight up the river into our faces. But we were dressed warmly, and the wind didn't matter much, at least not yet. The force that mattered, that surrounded us, and inundated us with its sounds, and pulled at or shook or carried everything around us, was the river.

To one standing on the bank, floodwater will seem to be flowing at a terrific rate. People who are not used to it will commonly believe it is going three or four times as fast as it really is. It is so all of a piece, and so continuous. To one drifting along in a boat this exaggerated impression of speed does not occur; one is going the same speed as the river then and is not fooled. In the Kentucky when the water is high a current of four or five miles an hour is about usual, I would say, and there are times in a canoe that make that seem plenty fast.

What the canoeist gets, instead of an impression of the river's speed, is an impression of its power. Or, more exactly, an impression of the *voluminousness* of its power. The sense of the volume alone has come to me when, swimming in the summertime, I have submerged mouth and nose so that the plane of the water spread away from the lower eyelid; the awareness of its bigness that comes then is almost intolerable; one feels how falsely assuring it is to look down on the river, as we usually do. The sense of the power of it came to me one day in my boyhood when I attempted to swim ashore in a swift current, pulling an overturned rowboat. To check the downstream course of the boat I tried grabbing hold of the partly submerged willows along the shore with my free hand, and was repeatedly pulled under as the willows bent, and then torn loose. My arms stretched between the boat and the willow branch might have been sewing threads for all the holding they could do. It was the first time I realized that there could be circumstances in which my life would count for nothing, absolutely nothing—and I have never needed to learn that again.

Sitting in a canoe, riding the back of the flooding river as it flows down into a bend, and turns, the currents racing and crashing among the trees along the outside shore, and flows on, one senses the volume and the power all together. The sophistications of our age do not mitigate the impression. To some degree it remains unimaginable, as is suggested by the memory's recurrent failure to hold on to it. It can never be remembered as wild as it is, and so each new experience of it bears some of the shock of surprise. It would take the mind of a god to watch it as it changes and not be surprised.

These long views that one gets coming down it show it to move majestically. It is stately. It has something of the stylized grandeur and awesomeness of royalty in Sophoclean tragedy. But as one watches, there emanates from it too, an insinuation of darkness, implacability, horror. And the nearer look tends to confirm this. Contained and borne in the singular large movements are hundreds of smaller ones: eddies and whirlpools, turnings this way and that, cross-currents rushing out from the shores into the channel. One must simplify it in order to speak of it. One probably simplifies it in some way in order to look at it.

There is something deeply horrifying about it, roused. Not, I think, because it is inhuman, alien to us; some of us at least must feel a kinship with it, or we would not loiter around it for pleasure. The horror must come from our sense that, so long as it remains what it is, it is not subject. To say that it is indifferent would be wrong. That would imply a malevolence, as if it could be aware of us if only it wanted to. It is more remote from our concerns than indifference. It is serenely and silently not subject—to us or to anything else except the other natural forces that are also beyond our control. And it is apt to stand for and represent to us all in nature and in the universe that is not subject. That is its horror. We can make use of it. We can ride on its back in boats. But it won't stop to let us get on and off. It is not a passenger train. And if we make a mistake, or risk ourselves too far to it, why then it will suffer a little wrinkle on its surface, and go on as before. ❧

WATER IN WILDNESS

"In wildness is the preservation of the world," Henry David Thoreau said, a remark which has been expanded upon by almost every "nature" writer since. In Islands, the Universe, Home, *a collection of her own ruminations on the federation of mankind and the natural world, Gretel Ehrlich reminds us that just as a flowing stream is itself shaped by the rock through which it cuts, wilderness and the human mind are an interactive continuum.* —P. S.

Excerpts from *Islands, the Universe, Home* by

GRETEL EHRLICH

It's morning in the Absaroka Mountains. The word *absaroka* means "raven" in the Crow language, though I've seen no ravens in three days. Last night I slept with my head butted against an Engelmann's spruce, and when I woke, it was a many-armed goddess swinging around and around. The trunk is bigger than an elephant's leg. I stick my nose against it. Tiny opals of sap stick to my cheeks where the bark breaks up, textured: red and gray, coarse and smooth, wet and flaked.

I'm looking for the source of the Yellowstone River, and as we make the day-long ascent from a valley, I think about walking and wilderness. We use the word *wilderness*, but perhaps we mean wildness. Isn't that why I've come here, to seek the wildness in myself and, in so doing, come on the wildness everywhere, because after all, I'm part of nature too.

Following the coastline of the lake, I watch how wind picks up water in dark blasts and drops it again. Ducks glide in Vs away from me, out onto the fractured, darkening mirror. I stop. A hatch of mayflies powders the air, and the archaic, straight-winged dragonflies hang blunt-nosed above me. A friend talks about aquatic bugs: water beetles, spinners, assassin bugs, and one that hatches, mates, and dies in a total life span of two hours. At the end of the meadow, the lake drains

27

into a fast-moving creek. I quicken my pace and trudge upward. Walking is almost an ambulation of mind. The human armor of bones rattles, fat rolls, and inside this durable, fleshy prison of mine, I make a beeline toward otherness, lightness, or like a moth, toward flame.

Somewhere along the trail I laugh out loud. How shell-like the body seems suddenly—not fleshy at all, but inhuman and hard. And farther up, I step out of my skin though I'm still held fast by something, but what? I don't know.

How foolish the preparations for wilderness trips seem now. We pore over maps, chart our expeditions. We "gear up" at trailheads with pitons and crampons, horsepacks and backpacks, fly rods and cameras, forgetting the meaning of simply going, the mechanics of disburdenment. I look up from these thoughts: a blue heron rises from a gravel bar and glides behind a gray screen of dead trees, appears in an opening where an avalanche downed pines, and lands again on water.

I stop to eat lunch. Emerson wrote: "The Gautama said that the first men ate the earth and found it sweet." I eat bologna and cheese and think about eating dirt. At this moment the mouth frames wonder, its width stands for the generous palate of consciousness. I cleanse my taste buds with miner's lettuce and stream water and try to imagine what kinds of sweetness the earth provides: the taste of glacial flour or the mineral taste of basalt, the fresh and foul bouquets of rivers, the desiccated, stinging flavor of a snowflake.

As I begin to walk again, it occurs to me that this notion of eating the earth is not about gluttony but about unconditional love, an acceptance of whatever taste comes across my tongue: flesh, wine, the unremarkable flavor of dirt. To find wildness, I must first offer myself up, accept all that comes before me: a bullfrog breathing hard on a rock; moose tracks under elk scats; a cloud that looks like a clothespin; a seep of water from a high cirque, black on brown rock, raining down from the brain of the world.

At treeline, a bird song stops. I'm lifted into a movement of music with no particular notes, only windsounds becoming watersounds, becoming windsounds. Above, a cornice crowns a ridge and melts into a teal and turquoise lake, which, like a bladder, leaks its alchemical potions.

On top of Marston Pass I'm in a ruck of steep valleys and gray, treeless peaks. The alpine carpet, studded with red paintbrush and alpine buttercups, gives way to rock. Now, all the way across a valley, I see where water oozes from moss and mud, how, at its source, it quickly becomes a river.

Emerson also said: "Every natural fact is an emanation, and that from which it emanates is an emanation also, and from every emanation is a new emanation." The ooze, the source of a great river, is now a white chute tumbling over brown bellies of conglomerate rock. Wind throws sheets of water to another part of the mountainside; soft earth gives way under my feet, clouds spill upward and spit rain. Isn't everything redolent with loss, with momentary radiance, a coming to different ground? Stone basins catch the waterfall, spill it again; thoughts and desires strung together are laddered down.

I see where meltwater is split by rock—half going west to the Pacific, the other going east to the Atlantic—for this is the Continental Divide. Down the other side, the air I gulp feels softer. Ice bridges the creek, then, when night comes but before the full moon, falling stars have the same look as water falling against the rock of night.

To rise above treeline is to go above thought, and after, the descent back into bird song, bog orchids, willows, and firs is to sink into the preliterate parts of ourselves. It is to forget discontent, undisciplined needs. Here, the world is only space, raw loneliness, green valleys hung vertically. Losing myself to it—if I can—I do not fall . . . or if I do, I'm only another cataract of water.

Wildness has no conditions, no sure routes, no peaks or goals, no source that is not instantly becoming something more than itself, then letting go of that, always becoming. It cannot be stripped to its complexity by CAT scan or telescope. Rather, it is a many-pointed truth, almost a bluntness, a sudden essence like the wild strawberries strung on scarlet runners under my feet. For half a mile, on hands and knees, I eat and eat. Wildness is source and fruition at once, as if this river circled round, mouth eating tail and tail eating source.

Now I am camped among trees again. Four yearling moose, their chestnut coats shiny from a summer's diet of willow shoots, tramp past my bedroll and drink from a spring that issues sulfurous water. The ooze, the white chute, the narrow stream—now almost a river—joins this small spring and slows into skinny oxbows and deep pools before breaking again on rock, down a stepladder of sequined riffles.

To trace the history of a river or a raindrop, as John Muir would have done, is also to trace the history of the soul, the history of the mind descending and arising in the body. In both, we constantly seek and stumble on divinity, which, like the cornice feeding the lake, and the spring becoming a waterfall, feeds, spills, falls, and feeds itself over and over again. ❧

WHITE-WATER WARRIOR

I have run most of the major rivers in the West more than once and lived to tell the tales. But unlike writers whose more reverent prose abounds with the peace and tranquility of western rivers, the magic of pristine campsites on sandy beaches fringed by cottonwoods and alder, the thrills and chills of white-water river rafting, I've been known to plant tongue firmly in cheek now and then and turn those images upside down, to tell it like it really is. . . . —P. S.

Snaggletooth by
PAGE STEGNER

Snaggle-tooth (snag'el-tooth') n. 1. A particularly vicious, mean-spirited, ugly impediment in the lower right-hand corner of what appears to be a dramatization of organic brain disorder. 2. A rapid on the Dolores River in southwestern Colorado. 3. A tooth that is broken or not in alignment with the others.

Let us rendezvous in Monticello, Utah, and drive up bad omen Highway 666 to the misspelled town of Cahone in the vastly overrated state of Colorado. For this trip we'll not only need *cojones* but a life jacket that will keep our heads out of the water when we're unconscious. We'll need cold weather clothing and warm weather clothing, because we'll be undertaking a 2,500-foot snowmelt descent from alpine forest to slick rock desert down a fast moving, sidewinder river, and we'll need prayer mats for daily acts of devotion. Praises to Allah for our continuing lives. Praises to Himself for making the warm part of the trip still to come. I hate rivers where I get wet, and it's just a total bummer being hosed down every five minutes up here in the snow.

The handbills will tell you there's something for everybody on *El Rio de Nuestra Señora de los Dolores*—The River of Our Lady of Sorrows. Sucker punches like spring wildflowers, white yarrow, aster, penstemon, and purple daisies, snowcapped mountain peaks, sheer cliffs of Wingate sandstone, Anasazi rock art, Great Basin redneck rock art, zonal transformations. If you don't like Douglas fir and yellow pine wait for the piñon-juniper; if you don't like piñon-juniper, wait for the sagebrush and rice grass.

There are indeed photo ops around every twist of the Dolores Canyon, but do not be deceived by slick brochures from the adventure companies. They fail to mention the steep gradient, the fast spring runoff, the absence of eddies into which to slow a boat when you need to put ashore, the rattlesnakes, the rain/hail/snow storms, the icy water. And they don't tell you why that miserable viper of a rapid they refer to in ominous terms as the "infamous Snaggletooth" is so infamous. For good reason.

But let us proceed. Let us sit back and let the dancing waters carry us from our put-in. There are seventeen of us in four oar-powered rafts. Twelve are California college students on a "field study," four are guides, including me, my wife, Lynn, and Ann Cassidy, a professional pathfinder and the only one who knows and understands our Lady of Sorrows. There is a woman I met at a cocklty factail party on the campus where I teach who claims she is a proficient boatmanperson even if she is a bloody academic, and finally there is my wife's business partner, Alabama Joe, who can't swim. "The deepest water I've been in," he says, "is my bathtub."

Day One is uneventful, except for a late afternoon rain. The students abandon ship the moment we touch shore and disappear to set up their nests, ignoring my earlier, and perhaps overly avuncular, explanation of river camping etiquette (unload boats, set up kitchen, *then* attend to personal space). Each, it turns out at dinner, harbors a singular food fetish, and there are complaints registered about pork by-products in the beans, a lack of soy milk, unripened avocados, and no humus. I don't even know what humus is.

Day Two is equally uneventful except for a disagreeable incident at the breakfast trough where I resolve a dispute between two coeds over a green plastic plate that each claims belongs to her. The contestants pull and tug and upset my coffee cup from its perch on a log, necessitating intervention. As they watch the plate sail deep into the tamarisk across the river, both begin to cry. I am, moreover, chided for littering by several observers whose sympathies are misaligned. But I ask you, would Major Powell have tolerated insurrection in the form of petty squabbles? Would he have concerned himself with Park Service regulations in a time of crisis?

At dinner the vegans are joined by two wheat allergies and an *e coli* victim and skip the roll-your-own (flour tortillas, meat, cheese). The chocolate brownies baked in a dutch oven are consumed, even though they contain unspeakable wickedness. I note that we are still carrying a near-full complement of diet soda pop, and am told it is scorned because it contains phenylalanine. I'm sorry, but I don't know what that is either.

We will encounter the "infamous Snaggletooth" tomorrow, and Ann is reminded of other runs through that particular maelstrom. Since she knows from previous excursions that I have been observed to *over*row an obstacle or two, she cautions me with a tale about our mutual friend, Walker.

Allow me a moment to set the scene. The entrance to Snaggletooth is through a chute on the left side of the river, several hundred yards upstream from the tooth itself. That jolly fang is near the right bank, and must be passed on its right side, which means the boatman must ferry himself, passengers, gear, and half-swamped boat clear across the river in swift current. If he's lucky he just makes it and thumbs his nose as he squeaks past the tooth. If he's been lazy he either wraps his boat around it, or slides off on the left side over a pourover that flips him upside down. However, if he's been too adrenalized and Herculean he can wind up among the jagged rocks just off the right bank. Major bad news in here.

There were four boats in the Walker party. The first two did not clear the tooth and dumped. Capt'n Walker, mindful of their fate, rowed like a maniac and wound up impaled on those barely submerged rocks on the right. And sat there being thrashed by the current like a shoe in a washing machine. The last boatman, a fellow I'll call Rick, flipped before he even got to the tooth, and watched his raft disappear from a midstream boulder perch onto which he managed to climb— bootless and unhorsed, so to speak, and praying that Walker would come unstuck and float down to his rescue.

Walker, flailing around in the furious current, finally *did* break free and managed to maneuver himself close enough to the boulder so that Rick could leap in as he swept by. Rick leapt, disappeared from sight, then reemerged ten yards *behind* Walker, back in the river. What neither had realized was that the sharp granitic fangs that had entrapped the boat off the right bank had ripped its bottom from stem to stern. And so Rick got to swim the mother of all southwestern rapids after all.

Our third day is chock full of events, but let's review only two.

Morning: We wrap one of the rafts around the end of a house-sized rock projecting out into the river from the bank. The rock is undercut and the boat is plastered underneath with only its nose poking above the current. Gear begins to tear loose from the frame—duffel bags, spare oars, spare life jackets, a dozen oranges, the rocket can used for the crapper. Most is recovered downstream, but a lot of people are going to bed in wet sleeping bags tonight.

We take turns bouncing on the one visible part of the stern (or bow, who knows), and over time more of the tube becomes visible. The current wants to spit this thing out and be rid of it. Bounce, bounce, bounce, more gear floats free, bounce, bounce, bounce, and finally, with a big sucking *ffffluuumphh* the bugger comes loose. Alabama Joe falls off the rock into the river.

This would be farcical and entertaining, except that Joe suffers the same fate as the raft—plastered by the current against the undercut rock with only his upper torso above water. We can't exactly bounce on *his* tube to jar him free. Lynn has him by his arms, but he can't move his legs to help her try to haul him up, and to tell the truth, I'm a little afraid of her being pulled in with him. At which point I'm afraid it's *adios amigo*, pal, you're on your own.

Across the river I notice that a group of students from the earlier boats has gathered to watch what is becoming, by the minute, less and less comic. The water is ice cold, Joe is getting tired, and the current is slowly winning the tug of war.

Cameras, I notice with a flush of anger, are being readied to record this great event for posterity, and I wave my arms wildly at them in disgust. Either get over here and help, or beat it.

We get two people on Joe's arms and ask him if he can *slide* his legs against the rock. He finds that, one at a time, an inch at a time, he can. Like a broken bug he begins a slow, painful crawl ascent from under the abrasive rock, chattering, becoming hypothermic, his attendant rescuers doing their best not to dislocate his shoulders by overzealous pulling. He slips once, and we jerk him back. He rests, recommences the crab walk. At last he breaks free. Unquestionably he leaves a lot of his epidermis (not to mention any chance for genetic sequel) with Our Lady of Sorrows, but he adds a terrific dinner party anecdote to his repertoire, and keepsake scars on his kneecaps to prove it.

Afternoon: Observing Snaggletooth from above one better understands the dread a trapped fox must surely feel, held in the vice grip of an implacable force that is utterly indifferent to its kismet. Today, at whatever volume the river is flowing, no options present themselves as to the run. We must cross the river, pass the old "snag" on the right, get clear back to the left bank, and land in fast water on a small beach before being swept around a bend into another long stretch of turbulent froth which ends in an undercut cliff—very bad news for swimmers.

The chute through which one enters this incubus is a thundering trough of white water that looks like an open spillway during flood peak. The left side of the river is a rock maze of broken boulders and refractory holes all the way down past the tooth, impossible to negotiate, and the slot to the right of our featured monolith appears to be just about wide enough for half a kayak. I sincerely hope this is an optical illusion caused by angle, distance, and drop. Ann assures me there is plenty of room, reminds me about downstream ferry angles, and warns me once again about the perils of an overzealous crossing.

My customary load of student passengers decide they'll hike around Snaggletooth and meet me at the bottom. Me? Isn't anyone going with me? I need someone to bail when I fill up in the entrance chute. I need moral support, you quislings, I need trust and confidence, love . . . at the very least valium. "I'll go with you, sweetie," says my faithful wife. And Alabama Joe, bless his heart and a southern-fried upbringing, will not leave a buddy in his hour of need. "I'll go with you, man," he says. "What the heck, I've already done my turn in the river."

Now the only major obstacle to departure seems to be stark terror. My mouth contains the moisture content of a desiccated road apple. The limbs seem to work, though not necessarily in conjunction with commands from above. Lynn and Joe, like kindly guards assisting a beshatted prisoner from his holding cell to the electric chair ("Dead Man, Walking") lead me down to the raft and fasten the electrodes. Silently, they switch on the current.

Down the long tongue of the rapid and into the exploding flume at its apex we shoot. V waves detonate over the bow and swamp the boat as abruptly as God's own dipper filling a water glass. I retrieve the arm that has been torn out of its socket along with the left oar, begin frantically rowing across the current, screaming "BAIL" at the top of my lungs, torquing my neck like a pretzel to try to catch a glimpse of the tooth I know must be charging upriver to meet us. But it seems to have

been vaporized, can't see it . . . total whiteout here. "Let's BAIL, people! No time to be dogging it." Ah, the hat's over my eyes, no wonder . . . now that's better, there it is, miles to go, miles, way down river, no sweat, but Jesus I don't want to overshoot this hussy, better ease up or I'll be doing a Mike Walker here. . . .

I don't know exactly when it occurs to me that I am going to hit the Snaggletooth dead on, but the realization has more humor in it than fear. What's that old joke about the last thing to go through a bug's head before it hits the windshield? Its mind? Well, things are out of my hands now, kismet's in charge, and it's Ann's fault anyway, she got me so nervous about rowing so hard. Maybe she'll be down there with some throw ropes.

My last act as we pile into what I see, up close and personal, is just a gigantic fang of decayed granite is to pull hard on the right oar and spin us into the facinorous, crushing, outrageous hole on the left side of the rock, where an astronomical backwave performs the Heimlich maneuver on our little hypalon tub, and we are ejected like spattering gobs of steak fat into the great maw of *Nuestra Señora*.

Flushed out below the rapid after the spin and rinse cycle is completed, Lynn and I swim frantically for the little beach before we are swept around the bend. Joe, however, has thrown in the towel and floats listlessly in his life jacket, resigned and submissive. He understands now that Mother Nature does not conduct business in a court of law, that double jeopardy is, in fact, her stock in trade. Clearly it is his destiny to drown in the river of sorrows. He hopes he will be remembered fondly.

When the throw bag hits him in the head he has no cognitive awareness of its function or purpose. But he grabs it, clutches it to him, and, as he tells us later, finds a certain courage in the developing fury he feels toward those idiots on shore who keep trying to jerk it away. He's damned if he'll give it up.

Thus in anger do we redefine karma.

Days Four and Five return us to the tedium of uneventful floating, the boredom that chaperons tranquility. There's nothing to do now but stare at 200-thousand-million-year-old vermillion cliffs of Wingate sandstone, streaked by a manganese oxide called desert varnish, laced at every seep and spring with hanging gardens of fern and monkey flower, overseen from above by golden eagles and from below by great blue herons as Triassic as the canyons through which they cruise. Even the sun has come out to spoil the ambience.

Soon we will have to make decisions about the future. At Paradox Valley (named for the geological formation, not the contradictions of white-water rafting), Highway 90 crosses the river, and we have the option of taking out in a community known as Bedrock, or of continuing another four days to the confluence of the Dolores and the Colorado just above Moab, Utah. Considering our shortage of humus, soy milk, goat cheese, tofu, agar, and powdered sea kelp; and taking into account Joe's emotional reaction to Ann's portrait of the largest rapid on that lower section of river, State Line—described in the slick adventure company brochures as "the awesome and incomparable State Line"—well, the choice is clear. We're out of here. ✺

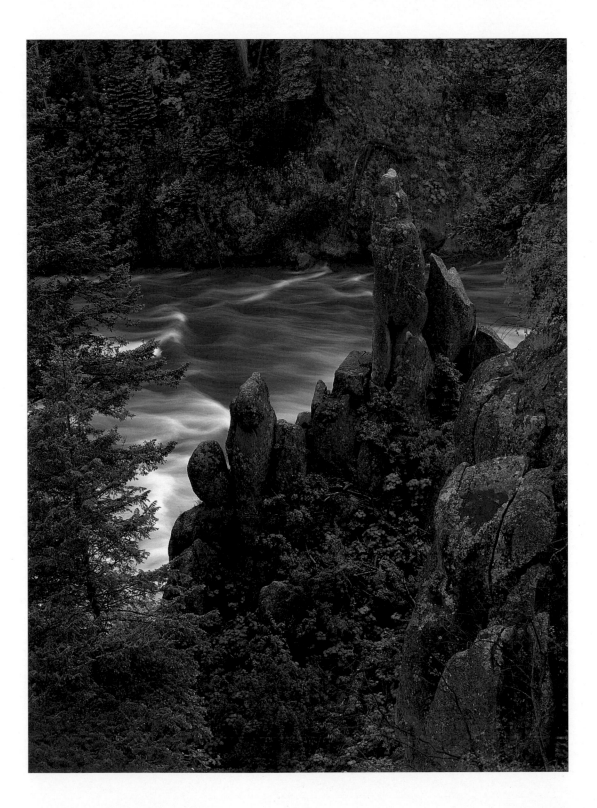

RIVER STONES

To many people a river, riverbank, and riverbed are merely part of the observed landscape, a bit of scenery eliciting an aesthetic response—or perhaps not. For Barry Lopez it is a book of revelation, a text that exposes us to the very fabric of existence. This excerpt is a chapter from his collection River Notes. *—P. S.*

Excerpts from *River Notes* by

BARRY LOPEZ

The overall impression here, as one surveys the river spread out over the gravel bars, is of a suspension of light, as though light were reverberating on a membrane. And a loss of depth. The slope of the riverbed here is nearly level, so the movement of water slows; shallowness heightens the impression of transparency and a feeling for the texture of the highly polished stones just underwater. If you bring your eye to within a few inches of the surface, each stone appears to be submerged in glycerin yet still sharply etched, as if held closely under a strong magnifying glass in summer light. An illusion—that insight into the stone is possible, that all distraction can be peeled away or masked off, as in preparation for surgery, while sunlight penetrates and highlights—is encouraged.

Beyond the light, a loss of depth, as the subsurface nears the surface, as though the river were exposing itself to examination. Kneel with your ear to the water; beyond the *plorp* of it in a hollow and the slooshing gurgle through labyrinthine gravels, are the more distant sounds of its fugue. A musical notebook lies open—alto and soprano clefs, notes tied and trills, turned notes, indications of arpeggio and glissando. Plunge your ear in suddenly—how it vanishes. Take the surface of the river between your thumb and forefinger. These textures are exquisite, unexpected.

Step back. The light falling on the dry rocks beneath our feet seems leathery by comparison. And this is another difference: the light on the dry rock is direct, shaftlike, almost brutal, so rigid one can imagine a sound like crystal lightly stung with a fingernail if it were touched; while the cooler light on the rocks in the water is indirect, caressing. This is why if you pluck a stone from the water and allow it to dry it seems to shrivel. It is the same as that phenomenon where at dusk you are able to see more clearly at the periphery of your vision. An indirect approach, the sidelong glance of the sun through the water, coaxes out the full character of the naturally reticent stone.

Fish are most exposed in the shallows, and so move through quickly. One afternoon I saw an osprey here, reminiscent of a grizzly at the water's edge anticipating salmon. A fish came by; he took off lightly and snatched it from the water.

Here, step across; you'll be able to examine things better out on the gravel bars. (We are fortunate for the day—temperatures in the eighties I understand.) Look, now, at the variety of stones. Viewed from the bank these gravel bars seem uniformly gray, but bend close and you see this is not true. It's as though at first glance nothing were given away. You could regard this as the stone's effort to guard against intrusion by the insincere. Here, look at these: the red, chert, a kind of quartz; this streaked gray, basalt; the greenish one, a sedimentary rock, shale, stained with copper; the blue—this is uncommon: chrysocolla, a silicate. The white, quartzite. Obsidian. Black glass. This brown, andesite. It's reassuring to hear the names, but it's not so important to remember them. It's more important to see that these are pieces of the earth, reduced, ground down to an essential statement, that in our lifetime they are irreducible. This is one of the differences between, say, stones and flowers.

I used to throw a few stones out into the river—underhand with a flick of the wrist, like this.

It is relatively simple, in a place where the river slows like this, fans out over the gravel, to examine aspects of its life, to come to some understanding of its history. See, for example, where this detritus has caught in the rocks? Raccoon whisker. Hemlock twig. Dead bumblebee. Deer-head orchid. Maidenhair fern. These are dry willow leaves of some sort. There are so many willows, all of which can interbreed. Trying to hold each one to a name is like trying to give a name to each rill trickling over the bar here, and making it stick. Who is going to draw the lines? And yet it is done. Somewhere this leaf has a name, *Salix hookeriana, Salix lasiandra.*

Piece of robin's egg, perhaps after a raid by a long-tailed weasel. Chip of yew tree bark, Fireweed. Snail shell—made out of the same thing as your fingernail. Here, tap it—or a rattlesnake's rattles. Roll it around in your hand. Imagine the clues in just this. Counting the rings would tell you something, but no one is sure what. Perhaps all that is recorded is the anguish of snails. Oh, this is rare: fox hairs. You can tell by the coloring. Some say it is the degree of taper, the shape. Up above someplace a fox crossed over. Or was killed by someone.

Behind the larger stones—let's walk up this way—hung up in their crevices is another kind of detritus entirely, a layer of understanding that becomes visible only under certain circumstances, often after a thunderstorm, for example, when the air has a sudden three-dimensional quality and it appears it might be slit open neatly and examined from the inside. What you see then, tethered to the rocks as though floating on the silken threads of spider webs adrift in the balmy air, are the sighs of sparrows passing overhead. The jubilation of wind-touched aspens. The persistence of crayfish, the tentative sipping of deer, who have stepped clear of the cover of trees, the circumspection of lone fish.

And there are still other revelations beyond these. You can imagine what might be learned in a place like this if one took the time. Think only of the odors, some single strand of which might be nipped between rocks, of wildflowers (lupine, avalanche lily, the white blossoms of bunchberry, yellow balsamroot, crimson currant), of musk (needle-toothed weasel, sleek-furred mink, bright-eyed fisher, grizzly bear on his rump, eating the seed pods of dogtooth violet), of suncracked earth, the odor of granite. Just so, by these invisible extensions is the character of the river revealed, is there some clue to what goes unexamined.

If you lie out flat on the stones—it seems odd to try, I know—you will feel—here, that's it—the warmth of the sunlight emanating from the stones. Turn your head to the side, ear to rock, and you will hear the earth revolving on its axis and an adjustment of stones in the riverbed. The heartbeats of salmon roe. One day I heard the footsteps of someone miles away, following someone else.

If you look up into the sky, straight up, eight or ten miles, it is possible to imagine the atmospheric tides, oceans of air moving against the edge of space in an ebb and flow as dependent on the phases of the moon. I believe lying here on the gravel bars cannot be too different from lying on your back on the bottom of the ocean. You can choose to take this view or not, with no fear of consequence. The tides go on, regardless.

Let's walk along the edge.

The fish this garter snake has just snatched is called a dace, a relative of the creek chub, a life more obscure than most. The snake is *Thamnophis couchi hydrophila*, a western species. You can take the naming as far as you want. Some of the most enjoyable things—the way the water folds itself around that rock and drops away—have no names.

You are beginning to shiver, but it's nothing to be alarmed over. The stones warmed you; you sensed you were nestled in the earth. When you stood up fear pooled in an exposed feeling around your back. This is what to leave the earth means. To stand up, which you see bears do on occasion. At the very heart of this act is the meaning of personal terror.

Along the very edge of these gravel bars are some of the earth's seams. A person with great courage and balance could slip between the water and the rock, the wet and the dry, and perhaps never come back. But I think it must take as much courage to stay.

I have stood for hours on these gravel bars. I have seen the constellations reflected in chips of obsidian glass. My hands have gone out to solitary willows in the darkness. Once I lay without moving for days until, mistaking me for driftwood, birds landed nearby and began speaking in murmurs of Pythagoras and winds that blew in the Himalayas.

I regretted throwing stones into the river. ❧

SHADOWS AND SILENCE

Great writing has the obligation to do more than just make us think; it must activate our senses and make us feel. The night Kathleen Moore describes spending in a driftboat on the coastal Oregon river is an excursion into pure sensory detail—or as she puts it, "pure feeling extended into space." Only in this kind of utter darkness, she suggests, with reflection and refraction under wraps, can we truly make a connection with the universe. — P. S.

The Night River by

KATHLEEN DEAN MOORE

On coastal rivers in the fall, when light is low and golden and the river pools up below the riffles, the water shines black, as slick as obsidian. Vine-maple leaves land lightly on the water, denting the surface, as if the flaming colors of the leaves were hot enough to melt glass. Between the Pacific and the riffles many miles upstream, the river stretches out in tidewater, rising and sinking twice each day, lifting the grasses gently and laying them down again, gathering alder leaves off the beaches and floating them in slow circles on the black lenses of water.

We launched in late afternoon on a slack high tide. The water was a perfect mirror to the cedars and swordferns bending over the river. Frank rowed on a reflection of a boat floating on the sky, boat on sky on sky on boat, the long oars pushing against their own images. Each stroke of the oars set the sky shimmering and lifted the smell of the water. When I leaned over the bow to watch for salmon, all I could see was the reflection of my own face, awash in the movement of the bow-wave. But as dusk came on and the river fell into shadow, I saw a golden leaf deep under water, slowly rolling end over end, and a dark shape darting away from the boat.

In the riverbed, the air turned cold. A mile. Another, and we pulled on our jackets. At the bend of the river, we passed through a pocket of warm air that still held the smell of fir trees sticky in sunlight, and I thought of the world we had left, a world of electric light and music. Color faded out of the landscape, the vine-maples darkening first, the yellow alders the last to go. Along the length of a willow thicket, we followed a shimmering wedge of light that we decided must be a beaver. The lines veered toward the bank and disappeared. As we rowed the last mile, a string of mergansers flew low over the water, beating upriver to some nighttime roost. Finally, at nightfall, we slid into a still pool below an island and dropped anchor. Silence settled around us like snow.

Pulling a knife from his pocket, Frank whittled the stub end of a candle and wedged it into the mouth of a beer can propped up on the bow. We poured tea by the small, wavering light and, perched on either gunwale, drank through clouds of steam. Then we spread our sleeping bags and lay on the floor of the boat in the dark, only a layer of goose down and the wooden hull between the river and our cheeks.

We weren't afraid, swinging from the anchor line in the middle of the river in deep pools of darkness, and we weren't tired, but curious and excited, like little children who are seldom out so late. Dusk is a borderland. The boundary between day and night bounces images off its shiny black surface, throwing back our reflections. From the interiors of our houses, we try to see outside, but all we can see are peering faces and the lamps behind. To see into the night, you have to wade into darkness, let it rise to your waist, your shoulders, over your head, until you lift and float, swaying, and night washes into your mind and presses against your chest.

* * *

The smells moved in gradually: in still air, the smell of damp grass relaxing, settling against the sand, releasing its vapors, its memories of the warm day gone by, the mud at its roots, the nests of willow leaves caught in its stems. When air moved softly downriver, the smells of river water seeped into the boat, autumn oak leaves and the roots of hemlocks steeped in water touched by spawning salmon. When warm air rising off the hills pulled sea-fret up the riverbed, I smelled salt and motor oil and the breath of fish, and iridescent piles of kelp torn from the sea and half buried in sand.

The sky came alive with stars, and Cygnus the Swan caught and turned in the white currents of the Milky Way, and Venus rose over the western horizon.

Waking now and then all night, we heard the sound of bubbles touching against the boat, a musical sound, like children playing far away. The tide passed out from under us, lowering us close to the glugging, fussing gravel bed. When it rose again, it lifted us with a sensation not of rising but of hushing, then, at high tide, of silence, the perfect silence of pooled water. From time to time, a salmon breached and fell heavily on its side, and then the boat rocked gently in the spreading rings. Again, we heard the guttering of water on wood. The boat swung on the anchor rope and the stars circled to the north, to the south, to the north, as if time had lost its sense of direction.

Without warning, a hard-edged screech. The violence of enormous wings beating the air. A terrible thrashing in shallow water that made the boat flinch against the restraint of the anchor line. I rose out of deep pools of sleep, my mind racing. A great blue heron? But not in the middle of the night. A bobcat then. Did a bobcat surprise a salmon? I sat up and looked over the gunwale: there was nothing to be seen but darkness packed densely into the riverbed. I lay back down. The movement of the boat faded away, faded away to dew-muffled silence and the *tap tap* of moisture dripping from alders onto the river.

Sometime after midnight, we awoke to find sea-fog rising in white flames behind the forest, silhouetting the branches of alder and cedar. The fogbank grew slowly until all the sky was suffused with white light that dimmed the stars. Something rustled in the grasses along the shore. When Frank shone his flashlight toward the sound, we discovered that we were caught in an invisible gale; in the beam of the flashlight, droplets swirled in little tempests, gusting and blowing sprays of dew, shooting skyward, then falling, then caught again and carried up by tiny tornado winds. Frank switched off the light, the storm disappeared, and all I could feel was moisture on my face, all I could see was the milky sky. I closed my eyes and the boat softened beneath me, moving as I moved, breathing as I breathed, quietly, slowly, damp and warm.

* * *

At night, the boundaries of our bodies fade into darkness and we become pure feeling extended into space. The substance of the world fades too, leaving only sense impressions—the sweetness of the trees, the dampness of the air. Lying in the boat, I am perception and speculation linked by moving air to the universe. A cedar dissolves into scent and washes into my mind. An animal's call hangs, disembodied, above the river. Starlight falls toward earth and damps out on the moist surfaces of my brain. The river disappears, leaving only its sound. I float, rocking, on the sound of water. ❧

SIDESTEPPING DOWN-STREAM

To call Ann Zwinger a naturalist, or "nature writer" is to ignore what makes her work so special—real science combined with an elegance of language and the poetry of imagination. The essay excerpted here is from her award-winning Run, River, Run, *a naturalist's journey down the Green River from its source in Wyoming to its confluence with the Colorado in southern Utah .—P. S.*

Excerpts from *Run, River, Run* by

ANN ZWINGER

The river shines clear and sharp. We eat breakfast sitting in a thatch of grass. So tentative is the morning breeze that only a single blade moves at a time. Overlaid green on top, at this altitude and latitude, the grass is still brown beneath, even in late June.

The river rises a couple of inches during breakfast, covering but not destroying the bird tracks. The silt, in which they are impressed, bubbles gently where groundwater runs in. The sky is high overcast by the time we shove off. An upstream breeze brisk enough to tip foam off oncoming waves catches me in the face. In this light, the water turns tawny. The channel is reassuringly deep, showing rippled and wave-marked sands beneath. But within the hour, as we approach Kendall Warm Springs, the river shallows and becomes ominously rocky. . . .

The first time I saw these springs was on an August day, when it was logical for the pools to be warm, for daisies, small fireweeds, yellow monkeyflowers, brook avens, and cinquefoils to be in bloom. One expects green horsetails, mosses, and water spring beauty. The next time was in January, when the air temperature was nearly zero. These warm springs were a striking dichotomy, with snow and frost patterns juxtaposed with bubbling water and green plants. The snow looked freshly sugared from the hoarfrost that coated it. Every exposed dry grass blade near the pools stood

69

like a motionless banner, half to three-quarters flagged with frost. The springs provided ample water vapor, that crystallized on surfaces cooled below the dew point. The air sparkled with ice crystals. It was physically and visually breathtaking, the radiant gleaming surfaces alternately revealed and obscured by floating mists. At the edges of the pools the snow surface was shaggy and imbricated, hanging over the water like white cockatoo feathers. The mists sifted aside, the sunlight unfurled, lighting all the snow and frost patterns with a blinding clarity. Where the stonewort grew above the waterline it was frozen crisp and bleached nearly white; beneath, in the warmth of the water, it gleamed emerald. White patches of snow capped each rock island, looking like heaps of feather boas. A water ouzel pranced, dipping briskly, a slate-colored lagniappe for a winter day.

The water was pellucid. The small rocks on the bottom, patched with olive-green algae, looked like old Indian-head pennies. The water skimmed through small channels, wedged and scalloped on the surface. Inch-long fish slipped with the current, then swam back against it. Called Kendall dace, they are endemic to these pools, a species (or subspecies, depending upon definition) of the speckled dace that live in the river below, isolated by the rising terraces of marl that finally prevented a free exchange between the river and the warm-springs populations.

I followed the springs down to where they debouch into the river, sometimes breaking through the snow crust well over my knees. The water spread and fell as a shallow screen, tossing up fingers of spray that tipped off into flying balls, frothing down the spillway into a small black pool that the warm water kept open in the frozen river.

* * *

In June, from the river below, the runoff streams spread and pour over the edge in filaments, gathering together in curtains that flash across the ledge, over the marl-built caves beneath. Their rushing sound is lost in the roar and pound of the rapids. The upper Green is a vigorous river, dropping a thousand feet over the seventy-five-mile stretch below Green River Lakes, an average of thirteen feet per mile, such a gradient alone engendering swift flow. Here it is steeper yet, and we face a plethora of boulders, which very nearly form a breakwater across the width of the channel. And Kendall Warm Springs rapids are prophetically marked on the topographical map as "falls."

In smooth water the bowman is no more than a galley slave. But in rapids, to be in the bow is to be dripping wet, involved in more action than there is time to react to. In running rapids, the object is to keep the boat parallel with whatever current it runs in, and the only way to maintain control is to go faster or slower than that current. The first stroke *not* to learn for river rapids is the forward stroke, for this only impels the canoe into bigger trouble quicker, the rush of the current itself adding enough acceleration into disaster without helping it along. The most important strokes are the backstroke and two sideways ones called a draw and a pry. With a draw the paddle is put out directly to the side of the boat, blade parallel to the gunwales, and drawn in flat toward the canoe; it pulls water beneath the canoe and the bow slips toward the side upon which the draw is made. A pry accomplishes the opposite. Neither is a natural movement and in practice I add more water to the canoe than I do direction.

In a rock-garden rapid, such as we prepare to run, ideally the bow spots the rocks the stern often cannot see, draws or pries to avoid them with a nicety of judgment, for a vast displacement skews the canoe about, making it vulnerable to being caught sideways by the current, at which point the river makes the decisions. The stern patterns his strokes upon those he sees the bow make: if the bow pries, the stern draws to counteract the torque and keep the canoe aligned with the current—running rock-garden rapids has been described as sidestepping downstream. There is no time for verbal commands, and even if there were, they more than likely could not be heard over the roar of the rapids.

At this moment, the canoe looks very frangible and I wish I were back upstream reading about running rapids in a book. The penalty for hanging up on one of these rocks is a capsize. There have been times on the river when I have thought a good capsize was part of "writer's experience." But when I actually confront this white water, self-preservation comes first: these rocks look like bone breakers. I do not want to lose my duffel or drawing pads and notebook, or see paddles splinter or the canoe smashed. There are white-water canoes with a watertight apron, but we are running in a standard open canoe that can ship large amounts of water, immediately rendering it cumbersome and unmaneuverable. Mathematically, in a ten-mile-per-hour current (which is a good fast rapid) the force broadside on a canoe hung up on a rock can be up to ten thousand pounds. The swiftness of a flip is incredible, quicker than one's mind can react. No amount of intellectual awe at big figures prepares me for the emotional instantaneousness of that force and its power.

More apprehensive than experienced, more overreactive than precise, I miscalculate and draw too hard on the left. The bow barely ticks a monstrous rock but it is sufficient to break our controlled forward motion and the canoe swings broadside against it with a ferocity that nearly throws me out of the boat. Water piles against the boat from upstream. Pressure surges against the hull. The canoe hangs there, tilted, alternately wedging tighter and rocking loose, water rushing too fast and too deep for me to be able to step out into the stream. Why we do not capsize I will never know—perhaps it is because the canoe is loaded, giving it a stability that a lighter one does not have. But mostly it is because of Perry, who keeps his head and does precisely the right thing at precisely the right moment. Somehow he pivots the boat off and we slip free and ferry to shore. I am trembling so hard I can barely get out of the canoe.

But running white water is like riding a horse: if you fall off, you'd better get right back on. The water for the rest of the morning is fast moving but the rocks are neither so large nor so close together, the slope of the channel not so steep, and the water not too deep to stand in if need be. It is good running, great for confidence. I can see the rocks pillowing up in front of bouncing backwaves. The rhythm of manipulating the bow becomes an elation as the canoe skims by easily and safely, rock after rock.

As we swing close to the bank, a mallard hen springs out, followed by three golden-tan ducklings that rock and lurch downstream in an effort to keep up with their mother, and I don't know whether I am laughing at them or just for the relief of not having capsized, or the joy of being on this river, this glorious, beautiful river. ❧

THE OLD FISHIN' HOLE

A day spent fishin' the crick is the setting for this comic and reverent chronicle of the annual ritual that begins long before dawn on a summer's day and ends hours later in soggy satisfaction. This delightful chapter is taken from The Grasshopper Trap, *one of several books by humorist and naturalist Patrick F. McManus.* —P.S.

From *The Grasshopper Trap* by

PATRICK F. MCMANUS

Retch Sweeney is on the phone. "Want to go fish the crick tomorrow?"

"Oh, I suppose so," I say. "What time you want to leave?"

"Four sharp," he says. "You know the crick. The best fishin' is always at first light."

"Okay."

Note the casualness of the conversation, the hint of indifference. The tone conceals any hint of reverence for the proposed undertaking—to go fish the crick. But both Retch and I know that we speak of solemn and elaborate ritual. We are talking religious experience here, mysticism, transcendentalism even.

Yes, transcendentalism. What we hope to transcend is time—thirty, forty years of time, back to the days of ancient summers with the crick flowing through our fresh, untarnished lives.

Rituals must be performed with precision. One flaw, one misstep, one missed cue, and the spell is broken. I must take care tomorrow to do everything exactly right. Otherwise, my one day of fishing the crick this year will be ruined, and I will be left with insufficient mental, emotional, and spiritual resources to sustain me for the next twelve months.

"Where's my black tenner shoes?" I ask my wife.

"You mean those wading shoes you blew eighty dollars on? They're in your closet."

"Not those. The black tenner shoes with the little rubber ankle patches that are starting to peel off. The ones that are worn through on the sides."

"Oh, no! Don't tell me it's time for you and Retch to fish the creek again!"

"Crick," I correct her. "The proper technical term for this sort of stream is 'crick.' A creek is something entirely different."

"Well, your tenner shoes, as you call them, are out in a corner of the garage where you left them a year ago."

"Good," I say. "You haven't seen my fish pole, have you?"

"What do you mean? You have twenty or thirty fishing rods on the wall of your office."

"I know where the rods are. What I'm looking for is the fish pole. It's steel and has three sections that telescope into each other, kind of green and rusty. It's got the old bait-casting reel on it, the one that makes the horrible sound because of all the sand in the gears."

"Oh, that one. It's out in the garage by your tenner shoes."

Early the next morning I head over to Retch's. I have brewed myself a large vacuum bottle of strong coffee and constructed a delicious lunch: thick sandwiches of fresh homemade bread piled high with roast beef, cheese, and onion; a banana; an orange; two candy bars; and a slab of apple pie. It makes my mouth water to think of the lunch, nestled there next to my bottle of rich black coffee. There? Too late I remember the coffee is still on the kitchen table with my lunch next to it. Drat! Damn all kitchen tables, those incorrigible thieves of fishermen's lunches!

It's nearly six when I arrive at Sweeney's house, two hours late. He will be steamed. I ring the doorbell. Five minutes later Retch opens the door. He is still in his pajamas.

"Wha'?" he says. "What are you doin' here in the middle of the night?"

"It's six o'clock," I snap. "Remember? We're going to go fish the crick today? I've been waiting out in the yard two hours for you to wake up!"

"Good gosh, the crick! That's right! Look, I'm sorry. Don't be mad."

"Oh, all right. It's just that I have such high regard for punctuality."

Retch leaves and returns a few minutes later. He is wearing his rotten old tenner shoes and carrying his fish pole. There is a dried worm on the hook that dangles beneath a quarter pound of split-shot sinkers.

"What kind of leader you got on?" I ask.

"Twenty-pound," he says. "The usual."

"Good," I say. "We don't want any fish bustin' off. Now where are the worms?"

"Worms?" Retch says. "You was supposed to dig the worms."

"Oh, no! I dug them last year, remember?"

"Yeah, I got an exact recollection. I dug 'em. And the year before that too. Well, c'mon, let's go dig some out behind the woodshed. Grab the shovel. You can dig and I'll pick up the worms."

"Why don't you dig and let me pick up the worms?"

" 'Cause it's my shovel, that's why."

We go out behind the woodshed, I spade up half an acre of ground, and we find only three scrawny worms. The next day Retch will plant his garden in the area I spaded up, but he fails to mention his plan to me now.

"Hey, I know where we can find some worms," he says. "Over in my compost pile."

In five minutes we fill the can half full of worms from his compost pile. Odd that he didn't think of the compost pile first. Mysteries like this tend to nag at one's mind.

I suggest that we divide the worms between two cans, but Retch says no, we will be fishing together so we can both use the same can. Besides, he says, he has only one good worm can.

It is ten o'clock when we arrive at the crick and start fishing. As Retch says, ten o'clock is the best time to start fishing the crick, because the fish were expecting us for the early-morning feed and will now be caught off guard. I agree.

The crick, still fed by melting snows in the mountains, is icy cold. We rule out trying to wade it, which means that we must hurl our lines over the wall of brush bordering the crick on our side and listen for the splash of the sinkers hitting the water. No splash means the hook snagged on a branch above the water, where it's unlikely to attract fish. We make several casts without hearing a splash. We then decide to cross to the far bank, which has less brush. We will cross the crick on two strands of barbwire, the remains of an old fence suspended above the water. The trick to crossing a stream on such a fence is to walk on the bottom wire and hold on to the top wire for balance.

Retch bounces on the fence over the middle of the crick. He begins to lean forward, pushing the top wire ahead of him with his hands, the bottom wire out behind with his feet. "Hanhh hannhh hanh!" he says, but I am uncertain as to what this means. He reverses his posture and is now leaning backward over the crick. "Hannnhhh!" he repeats, but with no more clarity of meaning. He gives the top wire a vicious pull, and faster than the eye can follow, flips forward. His body is now parallel to the crick, facedown, about a yard above the water, straining between the two screeching strands of wire. "Gah gah gah!" He says. I cannot help but be amused by this marvelous acrobatic performance, but enough is enough.

"Stop fooling around," I say. "You're going to drop the worm can."

My admonishment comes too late. His belly sags toward the water, even though he makes a valiant effort to suck it back up. He now makes a sound similar to that of a dog tugging on a rag—ERRRrrrrERRR! Then there is a whir and a yelp, and Retch plops into the crick.

I knew he would mess around until something like this happened! "Don't drop the worm can!" I yell. "Don't drop the worms!"

Ignoring my admonition, he splashes out of the crick on the far side, his mouth spewing out a stream half crick and half profanity. This is a bad omen.

I walk around a bend in the crick and find a cottonwood log that a considerate family of beavers had the decency to chew down so that it fell from one bank across to the other. Many people do not like beavers, but. . . . Halfway across the log, I notice that the spatula-tailed vandals have maliciously chewed a section of the far end down to the dimensions of a toothpick! I try to retreat. Too late.

"Pretty fast moves there," Retch says. "The first five steps across the water you hardly sunk a bit. But that sixth step was a doozie."

"Very funny," I say, wringing out my hat while waiting for Retch to stop cackling. "Since we're wet and freezing anyway, we may as well just wade down the crick. I'm glad to see you didn't lose the worms. Give me a handful of them. I don't want to chase after you every time I need a worm."

"Whatcha gonna put 'em in?"

"Why, my pants pocket, of course. They might ice up a bit in there, but I don't think it will hurt them, except they might not be able to have any more children."

About noon, the fish start biting. Two of them, a small one and a big one. We put them on a forked stick and divide the rest of the day between fishing and trying to find the last place we laid the forked stick. Retch deliberates whether he should eat the big fish or have it mounted. I mention it will cost him ten dollars an inch to get it mounted.

"In that case, I better eat it," he says. "I don't have an extra eighty dollars."

We pass up the best fishing hole on the crick. I am tempted to try for a quick cast on my way past the hole, but I might break my stride. That's what fast, mean cows watch for, a break in the fisherman's stride, and then they've got him.

"Shall we—*pant*—try to—*pant*—vault the fence or—*pant*—roll under it?" Retch says.

I glance back. The nearest cow is fifteen inches behind us and gaining. "Vault."

We vault and land safely on the other side of the fence. Not bad for a couple of pudgy, fifty-year-old men. The few little pieces of us left on barbwire are relatively unimportant.

We slip down to the Old Packard hole. It is called the Old Packard hole because years ago someone dumped an old Packard into the crick there. My cousin Buck once drifted a worm through the broken windshield of the Packard and caught a big fat brookie out of the back seat. It is now late in the day. I think just possibly Buck's brookie's great-great-great-great-great-great-grandchild might have taken up residence there. So for my final effort of the day I drift a worm through the windshield of the old Packard. The worm drifts down into the dark water of the back seat. I twitch the line ever so gently. I wait. Perhaps there is no big fat brookie there, I think. Then, like a flash of lightning, it happens: I am struck by the revelation that I am never going to catch a fish out of the Old Packard hole. Retch and I give up and head for home.

Driving back to town, wet, cold, exhausted, bruised, cut, and punctured, with only two measly fish between us, we stare silently ahead.

"I kind of expected it would turn out like this, the way the day started," Retch says. "You forgot your lunch, I forgot to set my alarm clock, we had to dig up half the countryside to find any worms, we both fell in the crick right away, and then got chased by cows, all for two little fish."

"Yeah," I say. "It was perfect, wasn't it?"

"Yep," Retch says, grinning. "Just like when we was kids. Funny, ain't it, how after all these years we can remember how to do everything just right."

"That's what a ritual is," I say. "Doing it all just right."

Now my wife is shrieking down in the laundry room. After all these years, you would think she would know better than to reach into a fisherman's pants pockets, especially after he has just returned from performing a crick ritual. ❧

OF DREAMS AND RIVERS

The only things grander than the rhythm of a bright mountain river or the flow of rushing water are, perhaps, the dreams and memories and imaginings that have the power to carry us back to such scenes when we are most in need of the solace and respite offered there. The recipient of many literary awards, Harry Middleton authored a number of powerful, vivid books including Rivers of Memory *from which this marvelous excerpt is taken, before his untimely death in 1993. —P. S.*

Excerpts from *Rivers of Memory* by

HARRY MIDDLETON

Even when I am not in the high country, when the business of getting a living keeps me away from the rush and rhythm of bright mountain rivers and trout, wild country keeps me company. Rivers move freely in mind and memory, rivers that I have known and many that I have only heard of, read about, visited through the books and the stories of other anglers. I have generously stirred all these rivers into my imagination. Even if I never experience any of them first-hand, if I never fish the wild rivers of Alaska or Idaho, New Zealand or Labrador, it is important that such rivers, such wild country, exists. There is solace even in the dream of such places, such water, such fish. There is more than a touch of magic in wildness: just the possibility of it nourishes the spirit.

Many a time have I merely closed my eyes at the end of yet another troublesome day and soaked my bruised psyche in wild water, rivers remembered and rivers imagined. Rivers course through my dreams, rivers cold and fast, rivers well-known and rivers nameless, rivers that seem like ribbons of blue water twisting through wide valleys, narrow rivers folded in layers of darkening shadows, rivers that have eroded down deep into a mountain's belly, sculpted the land, peeled back the planet's history exposing the texture of time itself. Rivers and sunlight, mountains and fish: they are always there, rising up out of exhaustion, a sudden rush of sound and motion, a Wagnerian assault of light and shadow, hissing water, pounding rapids, chilly mountain winds easing inexorably into a requiem of distant rapids, a fish's silent rise, the splash of blue-green water over the backs of wet black stones.

These dreams of rivers and wild river country, of trout, often take me by surprise, producing mysterious, comic ballets of clonic spasms, a puppetry of haphazard muscular shakes and shivers as sleep takes hold, as dreams rise, pillaging memory, fashioning worlds not of fact but of desire.

More and more these days my dreams are of rivers, of wild water, water that carries me away. . . . Last night's river was nameless: only a wide bend, a shoal of fast water, a series of dark pools giving way downstream to rapids. There was warm sunlight coming in wide veins off the surface of the river. I could feel it against my arms and neck, my face. A cool wind blew among oaks and hickories. The river moved through a pinched-in mountain canyon dominated by dark, hulking, mineral-stained bluffs. The canyon's stone walls seemed to undulate with moving shadows. Above and below the dark pools the river was silver, marked by flashes and bursts of sunlight.

I was there, asleep in the blue sleeping bag along the bank, near the wide bend where the river was shallow and hissed as it moved over the shoal of dark stones. I was soaked in warm sunlight, dreaming a dream within a dream. And the bright waters pressed downstream, time's silver, coiled, two-headed arrow, life's medium, motion given depth and character and fat with indifferent fish hanging in the currents, life with jaws open and belly empty.

The dream emptied me out of the blue sleeping bag, demanded participation as well as observation. I could feel the pull of the river against my thighs, the sweet invitation to let go, the urgent appeal to give in, let the river wash me away, carry me downstream into undiscovered country—that distant margin where there was no plain distinction between land and water, sunlight and shadow, form, time, and motion.

One thing about my dreams of rivers—I never fall. I worked the water, walking slowly upstream, moving effortlessly along the edges of the dark pools, into the fast, shallow water, sunlight glinting off the green fly rod's ferrules. For some reason I was barefoot: the moss-backed stones felt as though they were encased in some sort of amniotic membrane. I have no explanation for why I was barefoot in the icy water except that there is an edged honesty to dreams: they are never less ridiculous than the life that goes on and on above the dream line.

This is not to say that dreams cannot refashion life, usually for the better. In last night's dream my casts were heart-breakingly perfect, my presentation uncorrupted allurement. There was wind, but no wind knots; tricky current, but no difficulty with drag; there were magical hatches, but no pressure to match them. As I recall, I spent the entire dream fishing a single Griffith's Gnat. Its appeal never frayed. In short, there was never, as there is in an angler's waking hours, any conscious thinking about fishing, only fishing itself: emotions, feelings, sensations, instinct, rather than technique and theory.

The fishing was close, the trout easily released. Each fish seemed to hold in the translucent water for a long moment before vanishing, dissolving back into water and light, a light that flashed with the purity and intensity of summer lightning.

Hawks rose on warm winds. From the thick woods, where the shadows were cold and black, came a thrush's plaintive song. There were dimples of broken water on the pool above me. Rings of dark water moving in ever-widening circles until they broke softly against the riverbank. Fish moving. Rainbow trout on the river. Salmon pounding the water. Cutthroat wrinkling through the middle depths. Suspicious, heavy-bodied, rapacious, slack-jawed brown trout on the bottom waiting for the light's decline, night's cloak of anonymity. Brook trout thrashing at the surface so that the pools looked like cauldrons not of boiling water but of roiling wild fish.

The dream and river were one, inexorably joined, so that they seemed to go on and on, even after both spit me out before dawn, cast me into that slow waking that is like a diver with the bends trying to recover from a binge of having gone too fast, too far, too deep, of not wanting the drunk to end, not wanting to resurface at all.

Each night, before pushing away from the typewriter, falling into bed, I open the window at the far end of the room. The cold air that gathers at the edge of morning is a good alarm clock. I wake in the room's dull cold light, the dream still glowing in my head, a hedge against hard times, whatever the day brings. I can feel myself smiling at my good fortune, the good fortune of having wisely invested so much time in wild country, so many, many years in the pursuit of trout and the bright, fast rivers they live in, demand, the good fortune of filling my memories and imagination with wildness, memories that sustain me, good times or bad, that will nourish me whether or not I ever fish again, will illuminate me whether I ever again feel the press of wild country or am left only with its mark on my skin, its legacy in my blood, its spirit moving like bright wild rivers through my mind. ❧

About the Photographers and the Photographs

R. Valentine Atkinson is an internationally acclaimed photographer who specializes in angling and sports photography worldwide. His work has appeared in *Esquire, Field & Stream, Gray's Sporting Journal, Newsweek,* the *New York Times,* and *Geo,* among other publications, and has also appeared as limited edition prints. Atkinson lives in San Francisco, California.

> PAGE 36—Raft on rushing water.
> PAGE 41—White-water rafting beneath mountain.
> PAGE 44–45—Raft entering rapids.

Gary Braasch has photographed major environmental assignments for *LIFE, Audubon, Discover, Natural History,* and the *New York Times* magazine, and has been been published in more than 100 magazines worldwide. Braasch is an active campaigner and contributor to conservation efforts throughout the world. He lives in Nehalem, Oregon.

> PAGE viii—Columbia River through clouds.
> PAGE 55—Water rushing over rocks.
> PAGE 58—Red maple and lake reflections.
> PAGE 62–63—Dawn mists. Green Lake. Whistler, B.C.
> PAGE 64—Dawn. Camden, Maine.
> PAGE 66—Maple leaves. Concord River.
> PAGE 86—Canoe beside Salmon River.
> PAGE 98–99—Mixed maples and oaks. White Mountains.

Kathy Clay has traveled widely throughout the United States capturing America's most spectacular landscapes and wildlands. She has been published in major photographic books including *On the Trail of the Desert Wildflower, Seasons of the Coyote, Shadow of the Salmon,* and *Yellowstone: Land of Fire and Ice.* Clay makes her home in Dubois, Wyoming.

> PAGE 21—Wooden row boat along New River.
> PAGE 42—Sandstone Falls.

Willard Clay is a former botany professor whose well-known photographs have captured the splendor of the United States. His work has appeared in such publications as *Arizona Highways, Smithsonian, Reader's Digest,* and *National Geographic.* His book credits include *Yellowstone: Land of Fire and Ice* and *Grand Teton: Citadels of Stone.* Clay lives in Ottawa, Illinois.

> PAGE ii–iii—Foggy sunrise. Big South Fork River.
> PAGE 4–5—Middle Falls. Burgess Falls State Natural Area.
> PAGE 7—Waterfall and boulders. White Mountain N.F.
> PAGE 13—Tree trunk along Fiery Gizzard Creek.
> PAGE 14—Small rocky pools. Manido Falls.
> PAGE 22–23—Fall color below Sandstone Falls.
> PAGE 24—Upper Mississippi River.
> PAGE 25—Sunset over frozen backwaters. Illinois River.
> PAGE 31—Grass patterns. Obsidian Creek. Yellowstone N.P.
> PAGE 35—Sweet gum tree. Great Smoky Mountains N.P.
> PAGE 46—Black Canyon. Gunnison National Monument.
> PAGE 53—Eagle Creek Falls. Columbia River Gorge.
> PAGE 67—Duckweed and iris.
> PAGE 74–75—Pool with leaves in fall color.
> PAGE 88–89—Sumacs along North Fork. Boquet River.
> PAGE 90—Flowering dogwood. Great Smoky Mountains N.P.

Kathleen Norris Cook is well known for her outstanding images of outdoor subjects, primarily of the western United States. The recipient of numerous awards, Cook has completed two of her own books, *Exploring Mountain Highways* and *The Million Dollar Highway,* and has contributed to a number of other magazines and books, including *On the Trail of the Desert Wildflower* and *Women in Wilderness.* Cook makes her home in Colorado.

> PAGE 32–33—Ohiopyle River Falls.
> PAGE 48—Rock and leaf study.
> PAGE 65—Trees and reflecting lake.
> PAGE 68—Beaver dam with reflecting autumn colors.
> PAGE 72—Reflection.
> PAGE 73—Fallen aspen leaves in whirlpool.

Jeff Foott has worked as a cinematographer and still photographer since 1970. He specializes in wildlife and landscape photography and is dedicated to environmental protection. Foott documents wild animals and landscapes in National Parks and other wild places. His work has appeared in virtually every major wildlife and nature publication, including *Audubon, National Geographic, Smithsonian,* and *Natural History.* Foott resides in Jackson, Wyoming.

> PAGE i—Water rapids.
> PAGE 26—Lewis Falls and autumn color. Yellowstone N.P.
> PAGE 96—Pond lilies. Yellowstone N.P.

Michael Frye is a professional photographer specializing in artistic and innovative images of wildlife and the natural landscape. His photographs have been published worldwide and have been included in such prominent publications as *National Wildlife, Outdoor Photographer,* National Geographic books, and in Audubon calendars. He lives with his wife, Claudia, and son, Kevin, in Yosemite National Park, where he has lived since 1983.

> PAGE 6—Mallards at sunrise.
> PAGE 16—Flooded aspen grove.
> PAGE 30—Trees along Yellowstone River. Yellowstone N.P.
> PAGE 76–77—Willow bush. Merced River. Yellowstone N.P.
> PAGE 97—Water reflections.

Jeff Garton has roamed and photographed the American West for more than twenty years. His work has appeared in many publications devoted to conservation throughout the country and in such books as *Grand Canyon: The Great Abyss, Canyons of Color: Utah's Slickrock Wildlands, Voices in the Desert,* and *Glacier and Waterton: Land of Hanging Valleys.* Garton lives with his wife, Melissa, in Tucson, Arizona.

> PAGE 47—Rock spire. Henrys Fork. Snake River.

JC Leacock is a large-format photographer whose images capture the beauty, grandeur, and intimacy of the American landscape. His work has appeared in such publications as *Sierra, Wilderness, Outside,* and in Audubon calendars, among others. Leacock lives in the mountain town of Nederland, Colorado.

> PAGE iv—Autumn colors on rock. Great Smoky Mountains N.P.
> PAGE 11—Talkeetna Mountains.
> PAGE 52—Left Hand Creek after a snowfall. Roosevelt N.F.

Tom and Pat Leeson have been photographing wild places and wildlife as a husband-and-wife team for over twenty years. From their home base in Vancouver, Washington, the Leesons have worked on assignments for the National Geographic Society and National Wildlife Federation. Their images have appeared in such books as *On the Trail of the Desert Wildflower, Canyons of Color: Utah's Slickrock Wildlands,* and *Yellowstone: Land of Fire and Ice.*

> PAGE 8—Alders along Dosewallips River.
> PAGE 12—Vine maple leaves.
> PAGE 54—Sunset reflection.
> PAGE 94—Wild grasses.

Wayne Mumford, a professional photographer, is also a motion picture location manager/scout whose movie credits include *The River Wild* and *A River Runs Through It.* His photographs have appeared widely in books and calendars and in such publications as *National Geographic Traveler, Sierra, Sunset, Travel & Leisure, Country,* and *Montana* magazine. Mumford lives with his family in Kalispell, Montana.

> PAGE 3—Swan River, Montana.
> PAGE 56–57—Snag. Flathead River, Montana.
> PAGE 87—Autumn colors. Swan River, Montana.
> PAGE 95—Nigel Creek. Banff N.P.

Londie G. Padelsky is a professional photographer whose work includes scenic landscapes from much of the western United States, particularly the John Muir Wilderness. Padelsky's images have appeared in *Sunset, Sierra, Audubon, Backpacker, Outdoor,* and *Travel Photography, Western Horseman,* and *Country* magazines. She lives in the mountains of the eastern Sierra near the town of Mammoth Lakes, California.

> PAGE 34—Umpqua N.F.
> PAGE 78—Pink sky reflection. McGee Creek.

Nancy Simmerman has explored the Alaskan wilderness for thirty-five years on foot, skis, sailboat, dogsled, and bush plane. She has photographed two large-format books, *ALASKA II* and *Southeast Alaska,* and her images have appeared in *Shadow of the Salmon, Women in Wilderness,* and in numerous magazines. She also coauthored the guidebook *55 Ways to the Wilderness in Southcentral Alaska.* Simmerman lives on Lummi Island, Washington.

> PAGE 84–85—Salmon fishing. Prince of Wales Island.

Keith S. Walklet arrived in Yosemite National Park for the winter of 1984 and has lived there ever since, documenting its grand scenes and subtle beauty. He has explored and photographed most of the continental United States and Alaska as well, and his work has appeared in numerous national publications, calendars, books, and posters, and was selected for inclusion in *Best of Photography Annual: 1995.*

> PAGE 15—Autumn along Merced River. Yosemite N.P.